WATER

EXPLORING THE ELEMENTS: BOOK THREE

SIMONE AKASHA NOFEL

Dedicated to my nephew, Jett.
Keep being brave and always follow your heart.

And to you, the reader.
Be kind, be courageous, and keep exploring!

Water© Copyright <<November 2021>> Simone Nofel
Place of Publication, Seattle, WA

Book cover design, illustration, editing, and interior layout by:

www.1000storybooks.com

For more information, email support@heartyandfree.com

Paperback ISBN: 978-1-957327-07-5

Hardcover ISBN: 978-1-957327-06-8

eBook ISBN: 978-1-957327-08-2

Library of Congress Control Number: 2022905579

BEFORE YOU READ:

Grab a glass of water.

Sit outside by a pond, lake, river, or ocean.

Take a deep breath.

I am water. I am what sustains life on our planet.

Humans need me to survive, and so do plants and animals.

I cover 70 percent of the earth's surface. I am oceans, I am lakes, and I come in many other forms, too.

I flow from mountaintops and crash down as waterfalls.

You can see me roaring like a river, and you can see me still in a pond.

I am what comes down from the clouds on a rainy day. Some of you might like splashing in the puddles I form with my many raindrops.

In the winter, when temperatures get low, I like to change. My flowing liquid can become solid ice when it is very cold. Icicles and hail are both frozen versions of me.

In some places on earth, like Antarctica, you will always find me in solid forms. There are icebergs and snow everywhere!

Your body's organs require me to function properly, so stay hydrated! Drinking water on an empty stomach is always best.

Please help protect me by picking up plastic and other garbage in your environment. Beach clean-ups can be fun to do with your friends. Think of all our ocean friends who need me to stay clean so they can survive and be happy.

FUN FACTS!

- I represent courage, intuition, spirituality, and emotion.

- In classical medicines, I am associated with the bladder and the kidneys.

- I am paired with the color blue.

- My common symbols are:

SUGGESTED ACTIVITIES
(ASK YOUR GROWN-UP FOR HELP)

Go for a swim in your nearby lake, river, or sea.

Dance in the rain and splash in all the puddles.

Play a game of "Racing Water Drops"

- To learn game setup with directions, visit heartyandfree.com/4kids"

Find more fun at heartyandfree.com/4kids

COMING SOON. . .

Earth | Ether |

Check heartyandfree.com/4kids for latest releases!

LOVE THIS BOOK?
DON'T FORGET TO LEAVE A REVIEW!

Every review matters, and it matters a lot!

Head over to Amazon or wherever you purchased this book to leave a review for me.

My heart thanks you!

Lightning Source UK Ltd.
Milton Keynes UK
UKHW051007090223
416655UK00004B/241